COMING HOME TO YOU

COMING HOME TO YOU

how to live a more connected, magical, and authentic life

CAROLINE BRITTON

Illustrations by Alex Jones

The information given in this book should not be treated as a substitute for professional medical advice; always consult a medical practitioner. Any use of information in this book is at the reader's discretion and risk. Neither the author nor the publisher can be held responsible for any loss, claim or damage arising out of the use, or misuse, of the suggestions made, the failure to take medical advice or for any material on third party websites.

Paperback 978-1-913590-54-3
Ebook 978-1-913590-55-0

The Unbound Press
www.theunboundpress.com

Hey unbound one!

Welcome to this magical book brought to you by The Unbound Press.

At The Unbound Press we believe that when women write freely from the fullest expression of who they are, it can't help but activate a feeling of deep connection and transformation in others. When we come together, we become more and we're changing the world, one book at a time!

This book has been carefully crafted by both the author and publisher with the intention of inspiring you to move ever more deeply into who you truly are.

We hope that this book helps you to connect with your Unbound Self and that you feel called to pass it on to others who want to live a more fully expressed life.

With much love,
Nicola Humber

Founder of The Unbound Press
www.theunboundpress.com

For Claudia and Harry

May you always feel the magic of
returning back home to you

CONTENTS

PART 1 - REFLECTION

Part 2 - TRANSFORMATION

Part 3 - MOMENTUM

I am here to tell you
that you can be so
grateful for what you
have but still feel
disconnected.

How to Use This Book

You can use this book in different ways.

You can read from start to finish, open at random pages for intuitive guidance, or simply use like an oracle deck.

A key component will be having a notebook and pen on standby to explore the questions or exercises that are given in most sections.

If you are a visual person, you may also feel activated by the artwork that is interspersed throughout.

However you feel guided to navigate this book, trust yourself.

You've been called to it, at this time, for a reason.

May you receive the messages that have been calling you.

Introduction

I wrote this book for me and for you.

For me, because it's a book I would have loved to have been available to guide me at a time I felt utterly lost with two small children and a full-on corporate job.

And for you because I know there are so many of us out there who feel the same – who have become completely depleted and disconnected from ourselves.

This book is here to guide you back to yourself when you have completely forgotten what that person feels and looks like.

It's to show you that there is another way to live and it's your cheerleader in unlocking your fullest potential.

In many ways, this book is a remembering, an awakening.

Everything I write, you know deep down within you.

These words are here to help guide you back to that truth.

Back to the truth of all that you are.

This is about your re-discovery of who you are beyond the titles, the labels, the conditioning and the stories.

It is about awakening to a different way to do life. To do you.

So many of us reach for excuses to save soul-searching for another day and go back to living in the comfort of our current world.

Because of course we could just start tomorrow.

But I want you to feel into this.

What if you are wasting this one precious life by pretending to be someone you are not?

By pretending to be happy, fulfilled, okay, on top of things.

By settling.

In the wrong job, the wrong relationship, the wrong way of doing life for you.

What if I told you that one of the biggest gifts you could give yourself and others is to stop, to listen, to feel, to connect in.

To be radically honest with yourself.

We live in a paradigm where pushing, fear, striving, external validation and disconnecting from feelings are 'normal'.

In a world where many of us have forgotten who we are. What we need. How we feel. What makes us happy.

So many of us are swept up in the default of pushing harder, working harder or striving for the next goal that we've abandoned ourselves in the process.

So many of us are making choices driven entirely by ego and fear.

It's time for us to be the generation that breaks free from these patterns.

So you can come home to all you came here to be and all you came here to do.

Welcome

And so it begins.

The journey back home to you and all you are capable of. A huge welcome to you.

For me, the way in which we truly unlock all that we desire and all we are here to do is through connecting in.

So much of our external reality is shaped by the stories we tell ourselves, our conditioning, who we decide to be and what we choose to do during each and every day.

Often when we embark on a period of self-discovery, growth, or healing, it can feel like we are being cracked open.

Like the parts of our heart which we kept hidden are finally there for all to see.

Often we find that the darker parts of us emerge to be witnessed and explored.

Old patterns, stories, and beliefs will call to be released.

There can be a heaviness, an unease, as we shift things for ourselves, our ancestors, the people around us and the collective.

Take time during these moments to be with what arises.

Remind yourself that it is safe and powerful to feel.

Prioritise tending to your inner world above all else.

Be boundaried around how this space within you gets to be filled up.

It's in the darkest of cracks, in those moments of opening up, that the light gets in.

Into the parts of us that have been closed and protected. Into the parts of us that have been unentered caves.

As the light permeates into the darkest corners of you, remind yourself this is safe. That you are safe and all is well. Place a hand on your heart and repeat this whilst taking a deep breath in and out. This will help you feel grounded in your body.

Go easy with yourself as you navigate this book.

There are lots of questions that you may never have asked yourself before or spent the time exploring.

Great change comes when we start asking ourselves questions.

And when we finally allow ourselves to drop within us and hear the answers.

A Letter to the Reader

Five years ago, I was putting my young daughter to bed and I had a moment which I often reflect on.

A moment that still makes my heart ache.

I was reading her a story but I couldn't concentrate – my head was just too noisy.

I felt consumed by a voice that was telling me how much of a failure I was.

How I couldn't do anything well.

How I wasn't a good mother.

How I was pretty average in the work I did.

What a disappointment I was.

And I felt shame.

I genuinely felt I wasn't good enough.

That I wasn't deserving of the adoration of this divine little being.

As I look back at the woman I was, my heart breaks for her.

How hard she was on herself.

How disconnected she was from the truth.

How stuck she felt.

The thing is that with those feelings came immense guilt.

I had things in my life that people dream of – shelter, food, money to buy essentials, healthy children, a good job.

I was acutely aware of my privilege.

And why should I, of all people, have anything to feel bad about.

But the truth is that story wasn't helping anyone.

And perhaps you identify with this, with the voice that tells you to get a grip, to appreciate what you have, to be grateful for your circumstances.

But you too get to be deserving of having your soul listened to. Of expressing your feelings. Of tending to your wounds.

I am here to tell you that you can be so grateful for what you have but still feel disconnected.

To hear that it is ok to feel like it looks good 'on paper' but be unhappy and desire change.

To hear that it is ok to live a blessed life but feel unhappy, unsettled and unsure.

All emotions are valid.

All of us are valid.

It is in our constant avoidance of looking at what needs to be felt, seen and experienced that we cause a disconnect.

You can feel blessed and still take time to do 'the work'.

The world will be a better place for it.

You will be a better person for it.

The ripple effect of this will be beyond what you can comprehend.

'THE WOUND IS THE PLACE WHERE THE LIGHT ENTERS' - RUMI

PART 1 - REFLECTION

Introduction

It's funny the little things we remember. Seemingly innocuous things that people say tend to stick with us.

For me, it was a comment my Mum made.

I was going about my usual day, multi-tasking with my kids, aged one and three.

Chatting to her in the kitchen whilst simultaneously doing hundreds of different things – feeding the kids, emptying the dishwasher, hoovering, picking up toys, responding to texts, checking work emails.

And my Mum said to me, 'I feel exhausted just watching you.'

And in that moment, do you know what I remember?

Feeling proud.

I remember feeling capable and on top of life, and what a compliment for someone to marvel at my energy reserves.

The thing was, I was the one who was exhausted.

Exhausted beyond the demands of young children.

I was exhausted pretending to be someone I wasn't in the corporate world.

By my people-pleasing.

Always saying yes.

The constant need to prove.

The overpacked calendar.

The goals. The demands. The pushing. The lists.

The prioritisation of everyone else's needs above mine.

It wasn't long after that I welcomed in a New Year.

And for some reason that I didn't realise at the time, I decided to commit to a three-week yoga intensive course.

This yoga course meant that I was to wake up at 5:30 a.m., scrape the frost off my car and head to my local yoga studio for an hour of yoga from 6-7 a.m.

Now, being totally honest, I hadn't chosen it for the exploration of self.

It felt like a challenge for my body.

It felt like another goal.

As I started the yoga course, I was all in my head. I was constantly comparing myself to others.

If I could push myself harder, hold the pose longer, try a bit harder, I would be better.

The meditative practice at the end felt pointless. I remember thinking, 'What is the actual point of this? I am not getting any stronger here.'

In these moments, I was preoccupied by the desire to get home so I could get on with my day, my work, my chores, my job.

Then a few days in, something extraordinary started happening.

My body started demanding my attention.

Aches came. I started feeling all the things.

Guilt, anger, sadness, grief.

I started seeing colours and auras, and I became aware of the whispers of something greater than me.

Then 15 days in, we did a particularly powerful yin practice. A gentle form of yoga where you hold poses for a longer period of time. A yoga designed to help you *be*.

I hated every minute of it.

But with each pose I felt a softening. A surrendering. An ache.

I remember leaving that class and feeling raw. I was grey. I felt like I was a shell of who I was.

The next day I came out in shingles down the whole left side of my body.

My feminine had finally had enough.

She was ready to be heard.

She was demanding my attention through a virus that was showing up down the left side, my feminine side, of my body,

As I was signed off from work for two weeks, I got up the next morning and tried to carry on, but something had shifted.

I was so deeply tired that I couldn't keep going.

I took myself to bed and slept for several days.

When I woke up, I heard a message loud and clear:

You need to STOP.

You need to listen.

Everything in your life is telling you something is off.

And for the first time in years, I did just that. I started listening.

It was then that things got really interesting.

SORTING THE ROOTS FROM THE WEEDS

SECTION 1:

Getting Really Honest With How You Actually Feel

When I finally stopped, I realised I actually wasn't ok.

In the run up to the yoga course, I experienced many physical symptoms that were showing me that I was far from ok.

A few months before, I had experienced a panic attack on the stairs brought on by a mistake I felt I had made at work, a heavy workload, little sleep, and my one-year-old crying for me as I walked back to my desk to keep working.

I had also been in the neurologist's office with pins and needles and aches down my side.

MRI scans had proved inconclusive, so I carried on.

It was normal for me to work 10 hours, juggle two children with my husband away, have back to back weekends where we hosted, drink too much wine, and then berate myself for failing to have any sort of me-time.

I tried pretty much everything I could to distract myself from how I actually felt.

I tried:

overworking

exercise

jam-packing weekends

fixating on working harder or getting promotions

the constant need for money and safety

wine

and my favourite: just being busy.

This was the best one for me.

The more I could do and push and hustle, then the more I could ignore what my body and emotions were trying to tell me.

And even when the anxiety and the panic and the heart racing crept in, I just pushed it down, distracted myself, worked a little bit harder.

And at no point did I ask myself – *Are you actually ok or how do you feel?*

At no point did I stop cracking the whip and decide to just be there for myself.

Because the truth of it was I felt lost and stuck and sad.

I felt like a failure.

PAUSE FOR REFLECTION

Many of you may not even know where to start at this point. You may be wondering, 'How do I tune into how I feel?'

So we start here.

Imagine you are sitting in a peaceful room that only you have access to. It is totally quiet, there is nowhere to be, there is nothing in this room but the most amazing sofa and view overlooking a place you have been that feels special to you.

There are no phones, people, demands, emails, TV, distractions.

Imagine yourself in this room and when you feel

ready, imagine looking into a mirror and ask yourself:

Are you actually ok?

What is it time to be honest with yourself about?

Grab a notebook and write whatever comes up.

It might be

I feel sad, tired, something feels off, or I feel angry, stuck, numb.

Then take two minutes (set yourself a timer on your phone) and notice how your body feels.

Is it sore, tired, tense, tight, or perhaps there is a sinking feeling in the tummy or heart?

Again – make a note.

We are simply observing, not focusing on solutions at this point.

What is it time
to be honest with
yourself about?

AND THE DAY CAME
WHEN THE RISK TO REMAIN
IN A TIGHT BUD
WAS MORE PAINFUL
THAN THE RISK
IT TOOK
TO BLOSSOM.
-ANAIS NIN

SECTION 2:

Beyond the Excuses

There will be a million different reasons why now is not a good time to do the internal work.

I should know, I had a million of them.

Perhaps you have told yourself you are too young or too old.

That it's not a good time.

That you are too busy or have too many other important things to do.

That you should be more focused on working hard to make money.

That you are too cool or too logical or too important.

That it's self-indulgent, over the top, a fuss about nothing.

That you wouldn't know where to start anyway.

My list for not honouring how I actually felt was long and compelling.

Yes, I wasn't fulfilled by my job or particularly kind to myself but ...

I had young children, a busy life, a job with responsibilities.

I had bills to pay, commitments to honour.

And quite frankly, what were the other options?

It's not like I was going to honour the dream I had of running my own business and give up a career I had spent 14 years working hard to build.

Not with money on credit cards and zero clue how to be an entrepreneur.

The thing is, that is exactly what I did.

When I was able to finally get honest with myself, I realised that my life had been built on excuses about why someone like me couldn't make the change. Why someone like me couldn't do the extraordinary.

It was far too risky, uncomfortable, scary and quite frankly, insane on paper.

I mean, what if it didn't work?

What if I threw away everything I had worked so hard for and then had zero money, I couldn't get a job, and I let my family down?

What if I was totally deluded, and what about the several examples I had where I had failed in the past?

Then one day something just landed with me.

Yes, I was scared of failing, but what was bigger for me was the fear of regret.

What if I woke up one day and realised my whole life had gone and I had spent it ignoring the whispers of my soul?

This was everything.

It was then that I decided in order to change my external reality, I had to change my internal one.

I had to do 'the work" on making big shifts – by shifting my beliefs, my thoughts, my identity, my connection to my power.

And those internal shifts have seen huge changes in so many areas of my life.

This is how I sit here with a seven-figure business and writing this book.

I became bigger than my excuses.

I became brave enough to face them. To challenge them.

I started leaning into my edges. The discomfort. The untruths.

I started taking radical responsibility for everything I was creating in my life.

PAUSE FOR REFLECTION

I want you to ask yourself where your excuses have been in the driving seat.

Write down every reason why you can't make the change you want. Why you can't be happy like you want.

Really go for it.

Every excuse you can think of about why you cannot have, change or live the most extraordinary life.

Let the pen take hold and then when you have finished making your excuses, ask yourself this.

What if I become bigger than my excuses? What might be possible for me then?

I find it really helpful here to look at one or two people you admire who have done incredible things.

Actively find out three big reasons why they shouldn't have succeeded (I bet they have them) and then ask yourself why them succeeding despite these obstacles would be any different from you.

Changing your perception of people you admire as being better than you is fundamental here.

What if they are not better, more talented, more deserving? What if they just became more devoted to what was possible for them, rather than what was not?

If they can do it, you can too.

LOOK WITHIN

SECTION 3:

The Signs You Are Being Called to Stop

For many of my clients and me, it takes the physical body giving up for us to stop.

Maybe you find yourself in a position where your body is calling out for you to listen to it.

To rest.

To be.

It is at this point that we tend to pull on a list of reasons why we are too busy to indulge in stopping.

That we have dependents, jobs, money to make, people to look after.

That it all feels just a little self-indulgent.

That really you should just be grateful.

However, I promise you the answer is not to just keep on pushing through.

Or to keep hiding.

Or fooling yourself.

It's to stop right here.

When I was in the depths of being totally disconnected from myself, I used to say to my husband, 'Everyone takes me for granted, no one listens to me.'

The truth is I was taking myself for granted.

I wasn't listening to myself.

Burnout is a very real thing and something that can often creep up on us.

If you are feeling exhausted, drained, overwhelmed, detached, negative, alone, frenetic, fatigued, or de-motivated, then those feelings are trying to show you something.

I have found it immensely powerful to take the time to honour what my body is trying to tell me.

We are not supposed to walk around feeling like this, half living whilst we ignore the very powerful signals our bodies are trying to show us.

PAUSE FOR REFLECTION

What is your body currently trying to tell you?

What is not working for you?

Why do you feel you always need to be busy?

What are you wanting from other people, and are you giving that to yourself?

SECTION 4:

Starting to Understand Why You've Been Conditioned to Always Be Moving

---

We have been part of a paradigm that has thrived off our disconnection.

A world that has been breaking because of our inability to feel what needs to be felt.

A world where we avoid being honest with ourselves at all costs.

A paradigm which relies on you feeling not enough.

A world that relies on you feeling that you have to prove and push.

So many of us are motivated by fear.

A fear of what could happen if we stop – stop doing, over-proving, pushing.

We are told that happiness lies outside of us.

That it lies with the achievement of certain goals.

So we keep moving.

From goal to goal.

From attainment to attainment.

Continually moving can be addictive. When we are constantly fixating on getting to another place, we don't have to feel.

We can busy ourselves with the demands of the mind.

We can fall for the classic trick that the next achievement will bring us the happiness, safety, and security we are seeking.

There are so many people in this world who have been conditioned to believe that time should be exchanged for the pursuit of the next goal. The next validation.

Who are so focused on getting somewhere that they miss the journey.

And society at large benefits from this.

Corporations benefit from this.

In this paradigm, we have created people who will move at all costs.

At the cost of their health, their life, their happiness.

We have forgotten that time is our most precious commodity.

We can't make more of it.

Yet we believe it's the money, the status, the accolades that are the most important.

This was the biggest thing that kept me disconnected. I was always on the move. I was always doing, I was always striving, numbing, or ignoring.

I believed that my value came from my success, my achievements, my promotion, my ability to have everything together.

From always moving.

PAUSE FOR REFLECTION

When you get honest with yourself, how much have you bought into the conditioning that you should continually move?

Are you always chasing the next goal? Why? What do you feel it will give you?

What have you been taught to prioritise and give value to?

Is this making you happy?

I AM ENOUGH

SECTION 5:

Understanding Not Feeling Enough

I want you to think about not feeling good enough.

Being totally honest with you, I've always been someone who has leaned towards never feeling quite good enough.

I would constantly look at others and put more energy than I would care to admit into thinking about why they were smarter or more capable than me.

My work for a management consultancy exacerbated this.

Now I look back, I can see it was the perfect Universal training ground for me. Since I didn't feel enough, I worked harder, took on more responsibility – often without the financial rewards – and tried to be something I wasn't. I tried to make my brain more data-driven and to become a thought leader on matters that required high data analysis.

All in the effort to prove to myself that I was as good as everyone else.

Now I look back and I realise it was a huge life lesson for me.

My detachment to who I really was – a people-person who relies heavily on intuition and emotion – made me really unhappy. I wish now that I had seen the power in being my authentic, true self.

The empath, the free spirit, the nurturer, the warrior.

The woman who has incredible insight and a gift to see beyond the facts, words, and actions and to connect people back to their souls.

The woman who has phenomenal instinct. Who knows her power to heal, connect and elevate people.

It is exhausting being who we are not.

It is exhausting constantly trying to prove we are enough.

And it's such a driver.

We long to be accepted, to fit in. We fear being alone or abandoned or criticised.

So we do what we can to fit into the needs of others.

This was the greatest act of abandonment that my thirties saw.

I was so motivated by my proving I was enough that I completely lost myself in the process.

PAUSE FOR REFLECTION

Where in your life do you not feel enough? Where have you picked up ideas you are not enough?

How has that driven you in your life so far?

How might things change in your life if you believed you were enough?

GROWING OUT OF YOUR COMFORT ZONE

SECTION 6:

The Role of the Ego and Fear

Most of us are unknowingly governed by the voice of our ego.

The ego is not who we are, but often who we think we are.

A part of us that wants to keep us safe and is there to protect us but often gets too big for its boots, makes best friends with fear, and then calls the shots on everything.

The role of the ego is to avoid anything scary. To point out potential danger – great when we were confronted with wild animals in the primaeval days but not so good when you are trying to connect to the fullest expression of yourself.

One of the things the ego doesn't care for is doing anything that takes us out of our comfort zone. It's then that it comes raring up.

When we want to make a change, shake things up, leave a situation that does not serve us or step out of our comfort zone, it loves to buddy up with fear and provide us with a long and compelling list about why it won't work and it's a move fraught with danger.

The ego can be a big part in what is disconnecting us from our soul.

It keeps us in our mind. In the limitations of now. In disaster-based future scenarios.

Quite frankly, it is a massive pain in the arse.

My ego called all the shots when I was in the corporate world.

It worked to keep me pushing so I never got 'found out'.

It stopped me from being honest with how I actually felt because, quite frankly, what was the point? It would be too risky to try anything else anyway.

It kept me on my toes for fear that if I stopped and surrendered to where life actually wanted to take me, then impending doom would of course be on the cards.

Many of us are very, very motivated by the voices of the ego and fear.

Take something in your life now you want to change, and ask yourself why you wouldn't or haven't.

My guess? You've got a list of fear-based stories and reasons.

Then before we know it, fear is governing everything.

Where we live.

How we show up.

The work we do.

How we parent.

How we love.

The partner we choose or the love we avoid.

For me, fear and the ego were just perfect for stopping me in my tracks.

It was the best get-out-of-jail-free card I had for not making the changes I wanted.

And I was happy to use it.

Never mind that my light was diminishing in the process.

PAUSE FOR REFLECTION

Is fear controlling your life?

What decisions are you making based on fear?

What changes are you avoiding making in case they go wrong?

One of the most powerful exercises I have found is to let fear or my ego write to me. To list all the reasons I cannot do or have what I desire. To really let it have its say.

Then once I have finished, I ground myself and let myself reply back from love. I let that part of me that feels a different reality is available to me to write back with their thoughts, feelings and desires.

Once you have done this, you have a question to ask yourself – you get to keep one letter.

Are you going to choose the letter from fear or the letter from love?

TAKING BACK THE POWER

SECTION 7:

Understanding Your Ego

I named my ego Linda.

Now bear with me – it is not as crazy as it seems.

Linda is a part of me that used to make most of the decisions with an iron fist.

She made A LOT of decisions about why I shouldn't listen to my soul and should suck it all up, be grateful and crack on.

Now, Linda means well, but really she's pretty limited in her view of life.

She's the woman who never relaxes.

She's the woman sweeping up under your feet as you try and relax, sighing and muttering comments under her breath about being lazy, or berating you for being surprised when you get caught off guard.

Linda really loves to pre-empt a disaster and is mightily concerned – and to be honest, haughty – about people who don't.

Linda really really didn't want me to set up a business. Write this book. Speak about my spiritual gifts. Leave my job. Take loans to invest in my company.

She certainly isn't a fan of me trusting and acting on my gut feelings.

Linda is certainly not into going with the flow, trusting in the unseen and being guided by her spirit team.

It's enough to have her drop her head into her hands and declare, 'So be it. Don't say I didn't warn you.'

Perhaps you can relate.

Perhaps you have your own version of Linda that is constantly piping up.

One of the most powerful things to do is to recognise their voice so you know when it is stepping in.

Recognise their default patterns, stories, beliefs and sayings so you can access more neutrality when you are making decisions.

PAUSE FOR REFLECTION

What does your ego look like, speak like, and act like?

What personality traits does your ego have?

How are they governing the show?

SECTION 8:

A Letter to Your Ego

I frequently write or talk to my ego.

Below I have shown an example of a letter I wrote at the very early stages of setting up my business.

At this point I had zero proof my business would work.

I had a gut feeling.

I had done a lot of work on shifting limiting beliefs about myself, but I still found that I had so much fear about things going wrong.

This exercise helped in quieting the noise and the fear – I hope it helps you see the power and importance of challenging this voice too.

Dear Ego (Linda) …

I know you have a million and one reasons why you think that I can't do what I want to. Why I can't create a business and life that truly lights me up. I know that you like to hang out in the past and attach to memories where things haven't gone my way, or I've not felt enough, or the story from that friend about someone you know who failed. I know you like to hang out with the media and the news about why it isn't a good time to do what I want to do. I know you like to buddy up with all my limiting beliefs, my conditioning, and my old stories about why I am just not the kind of person who will get this success.

I know you like to attach to guilt and remind me I should just be happy and grateful with what I have. I know you like to hang out with your favourite line of 'Show me the evidence, show me that it will be okay and then we can move forwards.' I know you feel safer when you default to control and lack of trust. I know you can always make excuses about why it's impossible. I know that you don't believe it can work or that I might fail, and you only want to protect me.

But it's too much. I love and value you, but I have to make a choice. I have to make space for something else now. For my soul, for hope, for unlimited opportunities. Because my soul wants to speak. Because she notices. She notices when my stomach drops when I am doing work that does not light me up. She notices how my light is dimming. She notices my desire to do good and to make a difference. She notices my passions and sees how it flicks on a light within me. She notices the expansiveness in my energy when I play with my dreams about how good this can get. She notices the power within me to create anything that I want. She notices how I want to live my life with total freedom to be who I truly am. She notices how I miss that carefree part of me. She notices how I light up with freedom. She notices how I intuitively know I should follow a new path.

She isn't interested in: doing things for the approval of others. Following the status quo. Keeping herself small. Dimming her light. Hanging out with fear. Confining herself. Listening to self-criticism. Honouring doubt and fear. Controlling. My soul is focused on LIGHTING ME UP. She loves to follow joy, magic and flow. She honours following feeling, trust and inner guidance over hustle, fear and control.

Ultimately, she just knows. All that I am here to do and all that I am capable of.

She makes a compelling argument too.

PAUSE FOR REFLECTION

What do you want to write to your ego?

How do you want to respond to that voice that is governing you?

Use this as an opportunity to speak directly to the fear and to start challenging it.

SECTION 9:

Thriving Over Surviving

When we ignore the calling of our soul, we tend to be stuck in the energy of surviving.

For me, each day felt like a whirlwind.

A time when I defaulted to autopilot.

Of course, there are times when survival is the only thing we can focus on.

This is usually due to trauma, an immediate need for safety, deep healing, and huge life changes.

The energy of focusing on survival becomes all that we can do at that moment.

But what I am seeing is that more and more people are holding on to the energy of survival as their permanent and constant state of being.

A focus on getting to the end of the day.

A focus on making it to the weekend.

A focus on waiting for a better day.

A victim of their circumstances rather than the leader of it.

Are you in that energy of waiting for a better time to thrive?

A time where you feel more certain, more reassured, more ready to allow yourself to reach out and claim all that you desire?

I did this so much when I was fearful about leaving my corporate job.

I just kept waiting. I just kept focusing on surviving.

Waiting for the excuses to finish.

Then I found myself doing it in my business.

Waiting until I felt more ready, more sure, more convinced that this pull I have to do something will work out.

And it doesn't stop there.

I found it when I sat down to write this book. Hire new team members. Step into the next level.

That survival instinct kicks in.

Is it safe? Is it reckless? Will it work? Why rock the boat?

And I haul myself back to this.

I am here to thrive and not just survive.

I am here to be in the present and to lead myself in this life.

I am here to seize the day.

And the fear that comes up?

That instinct to stay in the energy of survival driven by fear. By caution. By control.

I call it for what it is.

It is not mine. It's not my truth. It's not the essence of who I am. I've picked it up somewhere along the way.

In a world that often says …

That joy is secondary to caution.

That following our heart is secondary to doing the right and sensible thing.

That jumping with our arms wide out into the wonders of where life will take us is secondary to sucking it up and watching out for risks.

What if we have got it wrong all this time?

What if our priority was always to …

Feel joy, follow our heart, soul, gut, feeling. To throw ourselves with abandon into the day, to live for each moment. To thrive.

PAUSE FOR REFLECTION

Where in your life have you defaulted to surviving over thriving?

Where are you fed up with settling?

What would a thriving life look like for you?

Write down a day that encapsulates you living your best life, from the moment you wake up to the moment you go to sleep.

What are you doing, who are you being, and what are you prioritising?

SEEKING EXTERNALLY CLOSES ME IN
I FEEL EXPANSION WHEN I GO WITHIN

SECTION 10:

Seeking External Validation

As we grow up, we are taught to seek approval and permission from those outside of us.

We are told we can be good enough when we meet the criteria that society has set out for us.

When we are tough enough, successful enough, attractive enough.

We go through life forgetting that our enough-ness is innate.

It's a given.

It's a part of our blueprint.

The quest for validation from others is exhausting.

It's a trick. It never stops.

No matter how much success you achieve.

This is the time where we stop bowing to the expectations of others and ask ourselves what is truly important to us.

Where you take responsibility that you are the creator of your own life.

Every one of us is unique.

We have a different set of desires and preferences.

It is not the job of someone else to tell us what our desires and our truth are.

They are welcome to their version and we are welcome to ours.

You and you alone get to trust yourself fully with what matters to you.

PAUSE FOR REFLECTION

How many years have you wasted seeking the validation of others?

What if you were the one who validated yourself now? How might that change things?

There is a visualisation that I love to do where I imagine that I am being interviewed for my favourite podcast or magazine. In this interview, they ask me about the changes that happened when I stopped seeking validation from others and instead trusted my own desires and my own enough-ness.

I imagine the most magical story I would tell about what happened next in my life. I write about how all my desires came to fruition.

Use this section to do the same – what is the most magical story you can imagine creating from now?

SECTION 11:

Beliefs You Have Picked Up From Other People

Somehow along the way, you may have picked up ludicrous ideas.

Ideas that you are not successful enough, loveable enough, worthy enough, good enough, clever enough.

I want to let you into a defining moment for me.

When I was in the corporate world, after the birth of my second son, there was a restructure and I was given a new role.

I knew my new Manager wanted me to prove myself, and I wanted to rise to the challenge. I really went above and beyond – I worked late hours, I would feed my son and then work until 10 p.m. on a Sunday.

I tried really really hard to get better at data analysis and Excel, and doing things the way I thought things had to be done. I set my heart on proving myself.

Then one day after I had done a presentation to a group of senior management – and I had been wracked with nerves beforehand – she pulled me into a room and said something that really stuck with me.

'I wanted to give you some feedback. You tried hard in that meeting but are not really a thought leader. I would stick to operations and work a bit on your public speaking too.'

I came out of that meeting and cried.

You know that feeling when a bit of you fragments – it's like a wound, and you can feel how your light dims.

Your spark goes.

Then the voice of fear and the ego steps up and takes over.

You internalise it, and it becomes your reality.

It becomes a deep-seated belief.

The thing is, I took that statement as the truth. And I am sure that the Manager in front of me didn't mean to cause such damage – she was simply operating from her parameters.

But it stuck with me.

And every time I tried to explore the idea of setting up my business or writing my book, her words would appear, and I would shrink down.

Because how could I be a mentor, a guide, a speaker, a teacher, or a writer if what she said was true?

How could I start a business that relied on my ability to captivate an audience, to teach, to create new and innovative ways of doing things if what she said was true?

But the thing is, it wasn't true. I took her words and made them mine.

But beyond that, I took her words and made them fit into the belief I had that sat beneath all of it. I wasn't good enough.

How many other people's words have become your own?

How many old stories and memories are running the show?

Because this is key. And I want you to read this again until it sinks in.

You and you alone get to decide you are enough. You and you alone get to decide what life you want to create. You and you alone get to choose what is possible for you.

Because I want you to know everything is possible.

I want you to realise that you can make it work. You are enough.

I want you to challenge, ditch, and become unavailable for anything that tells you otherwise.

I want you to decide today that the damaging stories of others about what is right for you, what you are worthy of, and what you can have are not your own.

You get to become the navigator of your ship and decide which beliefs you keep.

PAUSE FOR REFLECTION

Get out a piece of paper and write down all the reasons that say you cannot create the life, business, income, body, relationship or anything else you want.

Then I want you to take your pen out and cross out everything that you are deciding to let go of.

I want you to activate one of your greatest gifts, the ability to choose which reality and beliefs you subscribe to.

This is the moment you take your power back.

OPENING UP TO MY INTUITION

SECTION 12:

Being Mindful of Only Valuing Logic and Reason

Most of us have been conditioned to value logic and reason over intuition and feelings.

To rely purely on our human five senses.

What we can see, smell, hear, taste and touch.

We are often fixated on using our five senses for what is in front of us right now.

We then decide that what we currently see is our only reality and nothing else is available to us.

We are constantly asked, 'What do you think?'

Rather than 'What do you feel?'

We go to the mind before the heart.

We go to fact rather than feeling.

The thing is, we are a product of this.

Logic and reasoning are wonderful tools. I love that I have this analytical brain that is fundamental in running a successful business.

However, what I have found is that when I defer to logic and reason alone, it becomes limited.

I like to see it like a board room.

Imagine that you are the CEO of your life (you are), and you walk into a meeting room and have all different viewpoints around the table.

You have logic, reason, fear, your intuition, your heart, and your higher self – all with their own place at the table.

Imagine walking in, getting the viewpoint of just logic and reason, and making a decision.

Our job is to listen to logic and reason but to go beyond what you purely think and listen to all the other opportunities to be guided.

Asking yourself – What do I feel? What am I being asked to look at? What are my desires? Where am I being guided?

All of these things are important in moving you forwards.

One of the most powerful tools I use is to ask myself what I feel, what my gut, my inner knowing is showing me first, and then I ask logic and reason how we might be able to move it forwards.

PAUSE FOR REFLECTION

What is your intuition telling you at the moment?

What is off? Not working? Desires to be changed?

Visualise walking into a boardroom with different parts of you that want to guide you. What do they each have to say?

SECTION 13:

Let's Talk About Self-Belief

Let's talk about self-belief.

How many times have we seen successful people and put them on a pedestal?

How often have we seen individuals do amazing things but told ourselves stories around their achievements?

It's something I see with my clients, and it's such a common theme for many of us. We create reasons that make us think we could never enjoy the same type of success.

But what if I told you that you could create that kind of success in your life too.

Perhaps you feel like you are imagining it.

The unshakeable feeling that you are here to do bigger things.

The intuitive nudges that you are supposed to be honouring a new and expansive path.

The guidance you get telling you something about a situation, a person or something you are supposed to do.

The inner knowing that you are powerful beyond all measure.

And then you falter. You falter because it seems ludicrous.

How can you possibly know and act on something based on a feeling? A whisper. A hunch.

Isn't it incredible, the depths of our conditioning.

That thousands of years of patriarchal constructs have conditioned us to detach from the very power that lies within every one of us.

So I am here to remind you of what you know already. What you feel right in the depths of your bones.

You are the power.

You are the light.

You are the miracle.

You are source.

You are one.

It was never outside of you.

The sooner we all wake up to this, the more powerful we become.

Because, imagine this …Imagine a world where everyone stops looking outside of them and they connect in with their power.

The same universal intelligence that:

governs the oceans

lights the sky

creates life.

It is then we become unstoppable. We become light. We awaken everything – the codes that are inside of us, the ascension that is lying dormant.

Then the alchemy happens. Denser vibrations to higher vibrations. Dark into light. *We* into *one*.

You are not imagining it.

You are IT.

PAUSE FOR REFLECTION

Write a list of all the reasons that you should believe in yourself.

Why is now the time to finally step outside of these limited parameters and to come home to all that you are truly capable of?

You are source.

You are one.

It was never outside of you.

DIVE IN

SECTION 14:

Falling Back in Love With Yourself

I want you to fall back in love with yourself.

I want you to see yourself with such love and compassion, not just when you feel like you are in your light but when you are in all aspects of your being.

When we connect back to ourselves, our greatest love affair begins.

We like what we see in the mirror.

We like how we show up in the world.

We accept our flaws and nurture all parts of ourselves.

If everyone in the world were able to see themselves with compassion and through the eyes of love, everything would change.

So it starts with us.

PAUSE FOR REFLECTION

Write a love letter to yourself and commit to how you are going to view and treat yourself going forwards.

Record it on a voice note and play it to yourself regularly.

Write a post-it note or set a reminder on your phone which says, 'What is the most loving thing I can do for myself in this moment?' Then make a commitment to do it – no matter how self-indulgent or over-the-top it feels.

When we connect
back to ourselves,
our greatest love
affair begins.

IT'S ALL IN YOUR HANDS

SECTION 15:

It Is All in Your Hands

Something that comes up as we consider taking things back into our hands is a fear of judgement.

You may fear as you journey back to yourself that you are going to be judged by others.

Perhaps you even judge yourself.

Take a moment to think about any judgment you are holding on to for yourself and others.

Towards others who might be different from you, have different views from you or who have perhaps hurt you in the past.

Go deeper and see where you are still judging yourself.

This is the time to see that judgement with compassion and to release it.

From now on, every time judgement comes up, say to yourself, 'I see you, judgement, I love you, judgement and I release you, judgement.'

It's not easy to do this work.

In this first section, we have delved deep into where and why you lost your connection to yourself.

Moving forwards, we will start looking at how we can move through this disconnection and start coming back home to ourselves.

As the reflections of the first section come to an end, we will start moving into more practical things you can do in Part 2.

For now, we take some time to observe the biggest things we have witnessed coming up and to be with the emotions that have arisen.

PAUSE FOR REFLECTION

What has been your biggest takeaway in Part 1 about what has driven your disconnection?

What has been blocking you from being truly connected to yourself?

What is the most honest thing you can admit to yourself right now?

Inspirational Story From a Client Who Has Done This Work

Written for *BALANCE Magazine*
by Deputy Editor James Gill

The sign of a classic Treatment of the Month is how many texts, emails and all those incredibly self-indulgent WhatsApp voice messages I send to friends in the aftermath. So apologies to those whom I've been bombarding with my enthusiasm for Caroline Britton.

With Caroline, there is no messing. Of Manchester stock, she cuts to the chase in our one-on-one. Straight in there; she wants to know what you really want. If therapy is about healing, Caroline explains, then a session with a life coach is about driving you forwards. Caroline's USP is that she's also a little 'witchy'. More on that later.

I respond, 'Well, actually, things are pretty good, thank you very much ...'

'OK, so, we both know that I don't believe you,' she replies without batting an eyelid.

'Well, there is one thing I'd like to explore (Caroline would make an excellent interrogator). There seems to be a pattern in my life where I'm the person behind the thing. I got into comedy more than nine years ago, and then became an MC – never the main attraction. Then I got into TV warm-up. Again, I love it, but again I'm the guy behind the thing. And at *BALANCE*, I'm the deputy editor. I have zero designs on being an editor, yet it's interesting to me that it continues the pattern.'

And we're off exploring my formative years, discovering why this is the case. I sob uncontrollably on more than one occasion as Caroline explains which key moments in my life have caused me to believe that I'm better off essentially hiding; it's a form of safety.

I open up further and admit how I wish more things would land on my lap. I have what I consider a hustler's mindset – I feel like I'm always on the chase, rather than things coming to me. It is, frankly, exhausting. Caroline points out that I need to remove mental blocks. If I can do this, then things will flow my way. How? Well, homework comes in the form of two letters: one is a letter from Fear. The other from Love. I can't recommend this enough; the catharsis proves stirring. The Fear Letter – written the next day – has to be set fire to, and my poor wife must wonder about the ones that got away as I return from the garden, box of matches in one hand, exuberant air punches with the other.

And now, as Caroline describes it, 'The Witchy Stuff' (her inbox, she says, is crammed full of witch emojis from delighted clients). With my hand to God, as I wave goodbye to Caroline, my phone rings. Would I like to work on a secret TV project? Yes please. I've since signed an NDA the size of the (old) Yellow Pages, so we'll leave that there. Several other opportunities land on my lap in the next few days, including a recent dream gig at the London Palladium (check my Instagram).

Now, with this sort of stuff, you're either in or out. You're Fox or Mulder, Kirk or Spock. But with Halloween looming, now might prove the ideal time to let things get a little 'witchy'.

PART 2 - TRANSFORMATION

Introduction

In the introduction section of Part 1, I talked about how things became really interesting when I started listening to myself.

When I was signed off from work, my life started to pivot.

It's a time I look back on and relish. It was magical in many ways.

Days were spent taking things slowly. I started to nurture my body with the right foods, green juices and slow and gentle walks. I spent my days sleeping, resting and reflecting.

When my kids were not in childcare, I was more present with them. I sat and cuddled. I truly listened to them. I had nowhere else I felt I should be.

And a great unfolding started happening in my life.

As I started to feel better and more connected to myself, I set about building what I have now – a seven-figure mentoring business and a global community, serving thousands of people through free and paid content, a life with balance, freedom, flexibility and travel. A life where I really like the person I am and am passionate about the work I do.

And this all started from zero.

Zero clients. Zero brand. Zero clue how to run a successful mentoring business.

So, where did I start?

Now that I had become witness to just how disconnected I was, I started to focus on a huge amount of transformational inner and external work.

I started to take my responsibility as the creator of my own life very seriously.

There was nothing I didn't look at, as hard as it was.

The first place I started was by releasing anything that didn't serve me and replacing it with thoughts, beliefs, feelings, words and visions that did contribute to where I wanted to be.

I immersed myself into a world where I continually held the vision of who I was becoming and the life I was creating. At the time, the biggest desires I had were for two things – a business that made a big difference in the world and gave me the purpose, freedom and abundance I dreamed of, and to move into our dream house. I could really feel the desire for a big space and garden to be able to host all our family events, to raise our kids and to nurture me and my business as I got my work out into the world.

At the time, my business was generating very little money, and I certainly wasn't in the position to be able to do any of these things. The business I dreamed of looked near impossible to my logical mind.

However, I committed to this vision of the business, life and house I was calling in, day in and day out.

I would take a walk every lunchtime and dream of the life I was creating. I would constantly dismiss anything that told me that it was not possible and instead focused all my energy towards why it was. In every moment, I kept choosing that it was only a matter of time before it all came together and that of course my dreams got to be realised. Even if I didn't know how.

I completely re-coded my beliefs, my stories and the way I viewed myself.

I went through everything in my internal and external world and knew that there was immense power in what I chose to believe was true.

My favourite mantras: Everything is conspiring in my favour and everything is turning out more magically than I ever dreamed was possible.

I went all-in on coding these new beliefs.

I explored everything – coaching, programs, money mindset work, healing, reiki, womb work, breath work, 121 mentoring, movement, sound, self-development books and podcasts. I trained as a coach, studied numerology, became a reiki practitioner, did Priestess training, spent huge sums of money on my own development. Anything I could to shift what needed to be released, taught me something powerful for my soul, and that got me in alignment with a new way of seeing the infinite possibilities available to me.

Then things started to happen. The synchronicity of events still blows my mind, where the perfect opportunity, workshop, press coverage, or client would show up. In fact, when I ran my first workshop, the owner of the bar next door popped in to lend me some glasses – little did I know he was the very man who would buy the house I currently lived in, facilitating the move to our dream house.

There were some obstacles too, and as I look back, I see these were fundamental for my growth.

All of a sudden, people started telling each other about the transformation that my work was bringing about.

More clients came.

Then high profile clients came – sports professionals, those in the public eye, CEOs ... then they told each other. My business grew.

A few years in, I really felt it was time for the dream house, but everyone said, 'Not yet'. The numbers didn't add up. Mortgage brokers, my bank manager, and my financial planning team all told me, 'Just wait two more years.' I remember being in meetings where everyone admired my ambition but said very clearly, 'It's not possible at the moment.'

But I held my faith, I kept visioning, and I kept focusing on it being available to me.

Five months later, we got the dream house. It came through a series of extraordinary and very unlikely circumstances.

It taught me that anything is possible when you come back home to yourself – home to your truth, your desires, your power, your innate ability to co-create anything you dream of.

Over this next section, I will talk you through some of the things that worked for my clients and me as I set about transforming.

The previous section was about deep reflection; this section is all about transformation.

This is by no means prescriptive; if it lands with you and you feel you should explore, then honour that nudge.

If it doesn't feel right for you, then honour that too.

This is not about getting it right or wrong – it's about trusting any prompts you receive to try an exercise.

The words are through me and for you, and I trust this lands with you exactly how it should.

I started to take my responsibility as the creator of my own life very seriously.

TUNING IN

SECTION 1:
Starting to Connect Back to Your Body

Quite honestly, I had never spent much time thinking about serving my body. It's a luxury that so many of us take for granted when we are fit and well. Often we feel a disregard or ambivalence for the very vessel that houses us.

When I was first starting to recover from shingles, burnout, and stress, I started to become much more aware of how my body spoke to me. What she could tell me.

The little nuances and shifts where she demanded my attention.

It's so simple but when I felt the call to rest, I rested.

When I felt she wanted a green juice, I had one. Slowly and intentionally.

When she wanted to move or stretch, I did so.

When she needed fresh air, I gave it to her.

When she needed to feel or release an emotion, I made space for her to do so.

I started to develop a newfound respect for the prioritisation of her needs.

I stopped seeing this prioritisation as something that was overindulgent and selfish.

How many of us feel bad when we take time for ourselves?

It's worrying that we can't see how everyone benefits from a more connected, healthier and happier us.

I then started to take it further.

I explored reiki, massage, acupuncture, breathwork.

And then my body started doing something for me. Something I had never noticed before.

It was in constant communication with me. Guiding me. Showing me when something was off. Showing me when something was very much on.

It showed me with a drop in my tummy where something was off – like the thought of going back to work.

It started expanding when I dreamt of changing my life and running my business.

It lit up with joy when I opened a self-development book or listened to a podcast.

It showed me where my energy was supposed to be going.

My body has now become my most powerful guide. She is my go-to navigation system.

I ask her, *How does this feel?* and use her as my compass to move forwards.

I ask her to show me when something needs to be released.

She holds huge amounts of power with the work I now do, the energy I hold for myself and my clients and how I receive powerful messages for myself and others.

EXERCISE FOR TRANSFORMATION

Write down and plan for three changes you want to make with your body.

Recognise it takes around 21 days to change a habit and ask yourself how you can stick to this long enough that it integrates.

Start tuning into your body and asking for him/her to guide you.

What is your body consuming in terms of food, drink, stories, beliefs, and choices, that it no longer wants to?

Start by asking what thoughts, beliefs, and choices you are making that feel constrictive and heavy in your body.

What thoughts, beliefs, and choices are you making or can you make that feel like you are being expanded and opening up in your body?

My body has now
become my most
powerful guide.
My go-to
navigation system.

CURATING A WORLD WHICH NOURISHES MY SOUL

SECTION 2:
Becoming Aware of Your Environment

My body was also helpful in showing me where my environment was dimming my light and my connection to soul.

One day, I was on a popular news-based online site, and I started noticing that my energy had completely shifted from when I first sat down.

I was feeling fearful, scared, and low-vibration, and when I took a moment to question this, I saw that I had been feeding off fear, gossip, and societal judgement of others for a whole hour.

It started me thinking, if I can use my environment to feed my connection back to myself, then what is calling to be changed?

So I wrote a list and went through it ruthlessly.

I stopped watching the news every day. I stopped consuming magazines and content based on the exploitation of others.

I watched what I listened to.

I started observing the people and the conversations that drained me.

I took my environment incredibly seriously and became very boundaried in how this got to serve my life.

I started to observe.

What made me feel good?

What nurtured my soul?

What made me feel like I was coming alive?

And what needed to go that was the opposite?

Our environment is everything.

It's what we watch, what we consume on social media, who we spend time with, what we put in and on our bodies, the items we have around us and how we look after and treat them.

We are digesting things from the moment we wake up until we go to sleep.

Often we don't ask ourselves how it is making us feel.

Are you really enjoying what you are digesting in your life?

EXERCISE FOR TRANSFORMATION

Make a list of all the things in your environment that drain you, cause you to disconnect, brainwash you, or lower your vibration

Then ask yourself what lights you up. What raises your vibration?

Start by swapping each of these negative environmental factors out for something positive.

I would also really recommend a big de-clutter here too, as starting with your physical environment is a huge factor in your wellbeing.

Where do you need to tidy or throw things away that no longer light your soul up?

Where do you need to get on top of bills, your cupboards, your clothes?

As you go through all the things in your environment, ask yourself, *Does this feed my soul?*

If it is a no, then ask yourself whether you want to keep it. Consider how free you might feel if everything in your world reflected your decision to take your environment seriously and have it feed your soul.

Are you really enjoying
what you are digesting
in your life?

BOUNDARIES ARE AN ACT OF LOVE

SECTION 3:

Re-establishing Boundaries

I started to slow down, listen, honour my body, and be more mindful of my environment and then something came flailing at me that I wasn't expecting.

There were some very important people in my life who did not like this prioritisation of me or the person I was deciding I was going to be.

And they started playing up.

As a people pleaser and someone who is incredibly loyal, this became a significant challenge in my life.

My complete burnout meant that my over-giving had ground to a halt. I could no longer be all things to all people at the expense of myself.

I had to come first.

And this took a lot for some people to get a handle on.

All of a sudden, two significant relationships in my life came to a halt.

I was met with aggression and blame, and then I was completely removed from these people's lives.

And honestly, it really, really hurt.

But this was the most powerful lesson I was to receive at this time.

Was I going to abandon myself like I had done so many times before and acquiesce to the demands of others?

The Universe was asking me whether I was truly serious about this connection back to myself beyond all other things.

And I was.

So I listened to them and, with love, stood my ground.

I refused to become a doormat for blame over the smallest thing I had once said.

With a heart full of compassion for myself and them, I said no more and walked away.

These new boundaries looked like:

Me saying no to things that I didn't want to do.

Me speaking my truth if something went against my values or felt out of integrity for me.

Taking myself out of situations where people continually took from me.

Refusing to be a punching bag for the wounds and projections of others.

Unapologetically voicing what I wanted.

Leaving environments or relationships that continually took from me.

Now, none of this came overnight but what I realise now is that in each moment, we have a choice. To stand in our truth and in our power or to give it away.

Niceness is very different from kindness.

You can be kind and still have boundaries.

I would even argue that establishing boundaries is one of the greatest acts of love for ourselves and for others.

EXERCISE FOR TRANSFORMATION

Write a list of what your new, non-negotiable boundaries are.

Make a plan to start implementing these straight away.

Remind yourself why you are doing this and how you are going to benefit.

I would even argue
that establishing
boundaries is one of
the greatest acts of
love for ourselves and
for others.

I AM SORRY. I AM SO
THANK YOU.
YOU. I FORGIVE YOU.
HANK YOU.
LOVE YOU.
RELEASE YOU. I RELEASE YOU.
LOVE YOU. I LOVE Y

SECTION 4:

Shifting Anger and Resentment

As we start peeling back the layers, we can start feeling anger and resentment.

A lot of unexpressed emotions can be brought to the surface.

There are likely many emotions that need to be felt.

I cannot recommend highly enough seeking the guidance of a therapist, psychologist, counsellor, coach, healer, or specialist to help you process, explore, and release what is asking to come up.

Throughout the next section, I will also be guiding you on techniques that have worked with me and my clients.

These are incredibly powerful and the work is often deepened by having someone else support you through this.

I have seen the most monumental shifts here.

Clients who have transformed wounded relationships with mothers, fathers, and partners. Clients who have released deeply held trauma around grief, abuse, and loss.

Clients who have allowed themselves, in an environment that feels safe to them, to release painful memories that were stored in their bodies.

So, let's start with anger and resentment.

These are such low vibration emotions that can consume us.

When I started connecting back to myself, there were things I was angry about. I had anger towards others and towards myself.

One of the most powerful things I did was to let myself express what I wanted to feel.

I started by connecting to that child in me that wanted to have a tantrum.

The part of me that wanted to say how unfair everything was.

But rather than telling her to be quiet or to get back in her place, I listened to her.

Because this is the thing.

Can you imagine how frustrating it would be if you started to tell someone you loved about how you felt, and rather than listening and holding space for you, they just said:

'Be quiet, get a grip, shut up,' on repeat.

Yet we frequently do this to ourselves.

When a part of us wants to be heard, we shut them up.

We tell them to get back into their box.

And we wonder why there is a part of us that feels totally unheard.

Below I have offered three powerful exercises for releasing anger and resentment. I recommend you do these in sequence and in the order I have given them.

If you feel like you need additional support, I highly recommend seeking the help of a qualified professional.

EXERCISE FOR TRANSFORMATION
STEP 1: THE TANTRUM

Let the inner child in you have a tantrum.

What do they want to have a tantrum about? What do they feel is really unfair?

The more unreasonable, the better.

You can write it down or say it out loud in a private and safe space.

Start with 'it's not fair that ...'

It's not fair I have to work in a job I hate to make money.

It's not fair that I have to do everything.

It's not fair I don't have any me-time.

It's not fair that my boss said that.

Now, the key thing here is to be what seems 'unreasonable'.

This is not a time to negate that voice or to reason.

Just let them be heard.

Keep going until that part of you feels totally expressed.

While that part of you expresses itself, repeat 'I see you, I value you, I accept you, I love you. You are safe.'

You may feel like you want to find a private space and move your body, throw yourself to the floor, hit a pillow on a bed, wail, roar – do what you need to until that part of you has been expressed.

This may be an exercise you want to repeatedly come back to.

STEP 2: THE HO'OPONOPONO EXERCISE

This is one of my absolute favourites, and I see the most incredible results with my clients when I do this.

I highly recommend doing this when you have a few uninterrupted hours to spare - this exercise can take much longer than you think.

The Ho'oponopono exercise is a traditional Hawaiian exercise used for forgiveness.

This exercise is a great way of forgiving yourself and others.

Step 1:

To start with, find a quiet space, and get out a notebook and pen.

Step 2:

Ask yourself these questions:

- What are the resentments and stories I've been holding on to?
- What resentments and anger do I have towards others or myself?
- What negative emotions, memories, and stories am I holding on to?

These can be BIG things or the smallest things. It might be when you weren't picked for a team at school or someone said something hurtful. It could be when someone took advantage of you or resentment you have picked up for people who seemingly have it easier than you. It could be from big life events or a previous slight – the key thing is don't overthink it. If it comes up to be released, then trust that.

Step 3:

Then take a moment to write down anything that comes to mind, labelling each thing with a number (so you may end up with over 100 numbers or bullet points).

Step 4:

Once you have exhausted everything that is currently coming up, go through each statement one by one and say with real meaning:

I am sorry.
I forgive you.
Thank you.
I love you.
I release you.

Once you have said each of these five statements above to the anger or resentment thought you are holding to, then ...

Step 5:

Use your breath to help release each statement and put a line through the statement to cross it out.

Step 6:

Repeat saying these statements (I am sorry, etc.) and putting a line through each number on your list, one by one, until all the points on your list have been released.

Step 7:
Once you have finished, you can throw the list away, burn it (safely) or soak it in water and release it.

Please note: if you have deep traumas here in relationship to others, I highly recommend also seeking the service of a trained professional to help you navigate this.

STEP 3: RELEASING THROUGH YOUR BODY

The last powerful step is to commit to a daily practice of physically moving any anger or resentment through your body.

Go in a quiet room alone and hit a pillow against the bed, shake your body, cry, roar (you can always go on a car journey if you feel you can't let loose at home – just drive carefully!). Just get it out. This can feel very primal but it is hugely powerful.

Our body holds on to everything and is instrumental in helping you deeply release.

One of the most
powerful things I did
was to let myself
express what I
wanted to feel.

SECTION 5:

Working Through Money Blocks

Working through money blocks is a big issue for so many people.

Like many of us, I was never taught to understand money as an energy that was neutral and was simply responding to me.

This meant that I continually gave my power away to it.

My fear of not having enough money governed so much.

I was even willing to exchange time, my most precious resource, in order to get it.

Now when someone first told me that money is just energy, I remember thinking it was one of the most absurd things that I had ever heard.

Yet when we grasp this, we discover that money is simply responding to us. Our beliefs. Our receptivity.

But many of us have been conditioned to constantly be in a state of lack when it comes to money.

Now, I could write a whole book on money mentality (and many have), so I will hone in on what has helped me most in terms of changing my relationship with money. I have also recommended some of my favourite 'shifting money blocks' books at the bottom of this section.

So, here we go. As we start, the first thing is to get really clear on how you view money.

Imagine that money is a person.

What do they look like? Feel like? Sound like?

Are they scary, kind, or ambivalent?

How do you view them? Be honest: If you were on the receiving end of how you speak about and to money, would you stick around?

If you were like me, you might think, *I cannot believe I view money this way.*

When I first did this, I saw money as scary. For me, it felt like a man with a briefcase who was stuffy, mean, and controlling. I felt scared about the thought of interacting with him. It felt like he had complete power over me, and he called the shots.

Ask yourself today, *How do I view money?* Can you bring it to life in the form of a person, and what does that tell you about how the relationship might need to be healed or changed?

Once you have done this and when you feel ready to make some changes, I would then move on to these top 3 tips.

1. Do the scary thing and get clear on where your finances are now. Stop putting it off. Look at what is coming in and going out. Ask yourself whether you are using your money how you want, make a plan for paying credit even if it is a tiny amount, and cancel direct debits that aren't needed and don't light you up. Make a plan. You might also want to sort your wallet and financial paperwork as you do this.

2. Be grateful for what you do have, even if it doesn't feel much. Find gratitude for the smallest things.

3. Pick some money affirmations and repeat them every day. I love 'Money flows to me easily' and 'I love money, money loves me.' The Ho'oponopono exercise I recommend above in section 4 is amazing for money too.

EXERCISE FOR TRANSFORMATION

As well as the exercises above, start immersing yourself in the brilliant teachings of these writers/coaches/money guides – see if any of these books speak to you and then start doing what they suggest.

I continually commit to this work and putting their teachings into practice. It's had a huge impact on me.

You are a Badass with Money – Jen Sincero

*Rich as F*ck* – Amanda Frances

Secrets of The Millionaire Mind – T. Harv Eker

The Science of Getting Rich – Wallace Wattles

The Game of Life – Florence Scovel Shinn

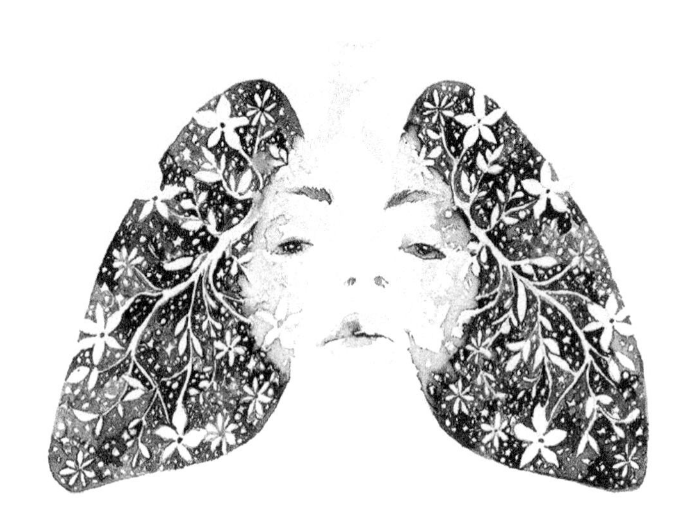

BREATHE TO RECEIVE

SECTION 6:

Self-Love – Learning to Receive

I never realised I found receiving difficult until I looked at it.

I was deeply uncomfortable with receiving compliments, support, and help.

I was the kind of person that if you picked up my kids after school, I would immediately feel bad and think about what I could do to return the favour and then some.

Many of us are not good at receiving, and it is causing us to block receiving in so many areas of our life.

We desire more money, more energy, more passion, more transformation, more love, more peace, and then as soon as we are given something that requires us to receive, as small as that might be, we say, 'No, thanks', and block it.

This was a huge realisation for me. I needed to show the Universe that I was ready to receive more.

Giving from the right intention is an act of love, and so is receiving from the right intention.

Take a moment to wonder how it feels to the other person when you disregard their attempts to give you something.

When people receive what we want to give, it fills us up. We vibrate higher.

The Universe is the same.

I have always seen the balance of giving and receiving like breath.

We breathe in and breathe out.

Things flow in and flow out.

I have found breath a really powerful tool in allowing myself to receive more.

Practice breathing in more deeply and imagining you are receiving more light, more space, more joy, more connection, and more abundance into your body.

And when you exhale, imagine you are releasing anything that is blocking you from receiving.

EXERCISE FOR TRANSFORMATION

Practice receiving. A compliment, an offer of support, love and guidance. Let that feeling of receiving land in your body – take a moment to receive it.

Set yourself a challenge each day – how can you receive today?

SPEAK YOUR TRUTH

SECTION 7:

Speaking Your Truth

Sometimes life demands of us that we speak our truth.

This means having difficult conversations.

With ourselves.

With others.

So many of us are blocked in the throat chakra, which is between the heart and the head chakras.

The throat yearns to speak, to scream, to sing, to express, to sound – yet it is not allowed.

The mind comes first.

It warns the throat:

Don't be too much.

Don't ask too much.

Don't express too much.

Don't allow yourself to be rejected.

Don't allow yourself to be truly seen.

And the heart responds:

But how will life know, they know, and I know if I don't express the deepest callings of me?

With real intentionality and love, we can let the words we speak, the sounds we make, and the activation of this beautiful energy body carry the vibration of our hearts.

As I have learnt to speak my truth, I have seen it change so much for me – the quality of my teachings, my writings, my relationship with others and with myself.

This is a time for you to find your own voice and to stop operating through the voice of others.

EXERCISE FOR TRANSFORMATION

Today, I want you to ask yourself what life, your soul, and your heart are demanding that you speak the truth about.

Start with yourself.

Where do you need to be honest?

Where do you need to honour a difficult conversation you need to have with yourself or others?

I would also recommend activating your throat chakra – sing, shout, groan, roar. Allow yourself to make sounds that your throat wants to make. Let your body guide your throat on what needs to be released. Yes, you might feel self-conscious, but we can do the hard stuff.

If this feels too much for you, I love the exercise of closing your eyes and visualising going into a room with someone who has upset you or where you know you need to speak your truth.

Imagine they are sitting on a seat in front of you and they never speak. Rather, this is an opportunity for you to get everything off your chest and to say everything you want to.

Once you have finished, you can simply declare, 'I hand this back to the Universe to be transmuted to the greatest and highest good for all.'

Then see yourself leaving the room and closing the door.

You can then open your eyes and take a big, deep breath out.

This exercise helps release some of the emotion you have built up so you can get more clarity and space within you to make a plan to move forwards.

This may or may not mean speaking to them in 'real life', but it is a great start.

The throat yearns to
speak, to scream, to sing,
to express, to sound -
yet it is not allowed.

AND SHINE
TO SPREAD YOUR WINGS
DO NOT BE AFRAID

SECTION 8:

Shining Your Light

Most of us do not like to shine brightly. To be truly seen.

We are uncomfortable radiating, being bright, and magnetising.

Often because it doesn't feel safe, or we feel it will make people feel bad, or it will mean we have gotten too big for our boots. Or that we may be abandoned.

How often have you dimmed your light?

Shone a little less brightly for fear it might trigger someone you care about?

Or maybe because you fear it will trigger someone you don't even care about?

You may be keeping yourself small and dimming your light to appease others.

Many of us have bought into this idea that we are too much.

This is often linked to a concern about what others will think.

It is important here that we look at where we are keeping ourselves small for others and why.

Often this can be because of the conditioning we have received through our peers, our family, and society about who we are and what is available to us.

But what if I told you that it is ok to shine brightly?

To be your most amazing and sparkly self?

There is no one else like you.

You are unique, powerful, and magical.

It's time to start owning that.

EXERCISE FOR TRANSFORMATION

Ask yourself where you have been resisting shining brightly?

What makes you feel radiant? Magnetic? When was the last time you felt that?

What does that part of you who loves to shine want to do, say, or be?

If you weren't worried about what people think, what would you do, own, or claim?

SECTION 9:

Liberating Yourself From the Past and The Stories of Your Ancestors

Many of us have received stories about who we are based on other people.

We pick things up from the people who raised us and the people who raised them.

We hold on to stories, beliefs, and conditioning from the ancestors who came before us.

Some of these stories can be empowering, some of them harmful.

In this section, I want you to become really intentional about the stories and beliefs that you want to keep hold of and those you do not.

A good way to start this is to look at the way you believe that life gets to be for you and how you view life in general.

It could be negative things like:

It is hard for me.

I am not someone who gets to be abundant.

It's greedy to desire more.

In my family, we don't have success like that,

Or positive things like:

I am so abundant and loveable.

Things always just manage to work out for me.

I am resilient.

Then I want you to go through those beliefs and decide which ones you want to opt into and out of.

Yes, you actually get to be in charge now of what you are actively subscribing to and what you are unsubscribing from.

This is where you can take your power back.

You get to decide which of the beliefs you keep and release based on what you have received from previous generations.

The most amazing thing about this work is how it is such a game-changer for the generations who come next.

Say you have come from a lineage where the belief is you have to make sacrifices to receive love or money, or perhaps there is a generational belief that you always self-destruct.

We store these stories in our bodies, in our coding.

Then, before we know it, we may have passed it on to our children.

We so desperately want them to be free of it and to know their enough-ness, but we don't believe we are worthy of the same thing.

You can break the cycles for the generations to come.

Do this work. Shift out the beliefs you don't want.

Our kids are looking at what we do, not just what we say.

What stories and beliefs do you want to embody for them?

EXERCISE FOR TRANSFORMATION

What beliefs and coding have you picked up from your parents or ancestors around the way life, money, joy, and following your soul gets to be for you?

Do you actually want to keep these stories?

Are they serving you?

Do you want to pass these stories down to the next generations?

What are you now being called to release?

You get to decide
which of the beliefs
you want to keep
and the ones you
want to let go of.

DREAMING UP MY IDEAL LIFE

SECTION 10:

How Good Can You Let This Get?

My medium, guide and friend of mine, Michelle Simmonds, once asked me, 'How good are you willing to let this be?'

At the time, I thought it was a bizarre question. Now, I believe it is one of the most powerful.

As we come to the end of this section, it is time to start opening up to the infinite possibilities that are available to you.

If you were to ask yourself, *How good am I willing to let this be?* What comes up? How big are you asking, claiming, and desiring?

This question helps me navigate past the *how* and brings me straight back to this fundamental truth.

Universal source energy is responding to whom I choose to believe I am and what I choose to believe is possible for me.

It's responding to my energy, my beliefs, and my choices.

There is no test that the Universe expects us to pass before allowing our desires to come to fruition.

Having what we desire come to us is natural.

How powerful is that?

The limits, levels, too-much-ness, not enough-ness, asking too much, *it is not possible, settle a bit lower, that's greedy, that's too big to ask* – these do not exist anywhere other than in our minds.

Universal source is not running things through a filter system saying, 'This desire is ok, but you are asking too much with that one.'

There is no such thing.

In the field of the infinite, which you are part of, everything is available.

So why are we not having all our desires coming to us whenever we want?

Because we get caught up in our minds, in our heads. We create stories around levels and worthiness and what is possible. We make certain desires mean more than others. We have a hierarchy in our head about this request being bigger than that one, so we decide it has to be harder, more laborious, more unlikely that we can receive it.

We get sucked back into the lower vibration paradigms and feel fear, guilt, greed, constriction.

We get obsessed with the *how*.

We stop the flow.

We block what could be easy.

I've been playing with some things in my life and business recently.

Predominantly, the simpler I allow it to be, the more it gets to be.

I've been asking myself these questions, and I share them in the hope they help you.

What if you just allowed it to be simple?

What if you forgot the things you thought you had to do to have what you want and instead, you allowed life, business, connection, and flow to be simple?

What if you were just in pure trust that it would work out?

So today, ask yourself – what do you actually want to happen?

What if everything you desired could be chosen? Are you choosing what you truly desire?

What if any way of being and living was on the table? How would you live day to day, moment to moment? What would you want your life to feel like?

And what if you just chose to take action from a deep-seated belief you get to have the most extraordinary life?

EXERCISE FOR TRANSFORMATION

What are your blocks for letting life be this good?

Where have you learnt that you are not deserving or that it is impossible?

What if you decided it was possible?

How does this change the action you might take?

Inspirational Stories From Clients Who Have Done This Work

I want to talk about the amazing woman that is Caroline Britton because I had one of the most incredible sessions of my life with her during the lockdown. I was definitely hanging onto quite a lot of stuff from my past about my Mum, stuff that came up from my childhood and also fears around death actually after losing my Dad. The way I was bringing up my daughter, I was really concerned that I was gonna make the same mistakes that I guess I'd been through with my own parents.

I'd never done a healing session like guided meditation or something similar to that before, although I am quite a spiritual person. I have never experienced anything on this level. I clearly had a load of blockages here (in my chest) and a load of unshifted energy. I had done some therapy but I just felt like it was just sitting here (in my chest). Caroline took me on this journey for over 90 minutes. I spent the majority of the time crying, but I released something inside of myself. I actually have been a different person since that session, and I have been shouting her name from the rooftops. She is an incredible person to work with if you are going through anything in your life. If you feel like you need help with some stuff, letting go, fears, relationship problems, stresses – she is the right person to call. I can't recommend her highly enough.

Zoe Hardman, Presenter

For the best part of 15 years, I worked in advertising and threw my whole self into it. Then in my early thirties I began to suffer with serious burnout that led to depression and in turn a re-evaluation of pretty much everything in my life. I decided to start my own business which went really well at first but then the burnout reappeared, and I knew I had to make some deeper more meaningful changes. At this point Caroline magically appeared in my life!

I first saw her talking at an event and knew she was someone I needed to work with, although I didn't exactly know how at first. So, I reached out to her via email, and before I knew it, I was sitting in her kitchen pouring my heart out to her. Gradually Caroline got me to get to the root of what was missing, which for me was my creativity. I'd always been a creative kid, and somewhat ironically, I'd gone into advertising because I thought it would allow me to further indulge this side of me, but sadly not. With Caroline's guidance, I began seeking out more creative work, which led me to start taking my photography hobby a little more seriously, and before I knew it, my business was entirely focused on photographing businesswomen. I was living my biggest, brightest dreams, and I'm quite blown away by what I've achieved since sitting in that kitchen.

The beautiful part of working with Caroline is the fact that we've been able to overcome some of our fears together. Caroline was one of my very first photography clients, which pushed both me and her out of our comfort zones. In further working with Caroline, I began to recognise my own fears around being more visible, in promoting myself and my business, and being proud of my talent instead of shying away from it, almost apologising for it. As I addressed this fear, I began to uncover my truest purpose, and now I help other women overcome their own fears about being seen. To put aside all the stories they've been told about hiding their talents, about judging how they look as more important than the gifts they possess. It's incredible work I now get to do with extraordinary women, and Caroline played no small part in that – in fact, she still very much does. Watching her growth has been such a privilege, and it spurs me on to grow, to expand, and to take away any limiting beliefs about what is possible.

Karen Staniland-Platt, With Passion and Purpose

PART 3 - MOMENTUM

Introduction

Looking back, I realise all the disconnection I experienced was not something that happened by accident; this has been a deliberate part of the plan. The unfolding of my purpose through the unfolding of me.

My purpose on this planet is to connect people back to the truest essence of who they are.

I witness so many people who are striving for success or who have the 'success' and who still feel disconnected from who they are. They've lost their sense of deep connection to joy, to life, to themselves.

With the work I've done I have seen the most extraordinary results with entrepreneurs, healers, lightworkers, doctors, lawyers, coaches, CEOs, sports professionals, parents, those in the public eye, and more. This work has had a profound impact on so many people. It is so needed by so many people.

Now that we have reflected on what got us to the point of disconnection and set in motion the transformational tools to bring us back to ourselves, I want to talk about creating momentum in your life.

I want to focus on building a life and a connection that truly lights you up.

If I can go from stuck, frenetic and burnout to free, at peace and deeply connected to my purpose, then I believe you can too.

Each of us has the power to create the most incredible reality.

And our most powerful tool?

The voice of the soul that resides within us.

By following her lead, I've seen the most incredible results. I've created:

a business with global impact

a seven-figure brand

a book that speaks from my soul to yours

a life which has balance and joy and connection

a family balance that works for me where I work between school hours and have the holidays off

a body and energy I love

a deep connection with who I am and the most incredible relationship with myself.

This can be your reality too.

But we start by deciding that it is available for us.

Then we choose it.

Every single day.

It's the moments that we honour the calling of our soul that really matter.

That has been my greatest realisation of all.

In this section, we are going to focus on ways in which you can get momentum and build the life you truly desire.

Now is the time to take radical responsibility for deciding what you really want and for making it happen.

SECTION 1:

Connecting to What You Really Want

So my question to you is this: *What is it you actually desire to have, be, or do?*

What are you asking for if anything is on the table?

What are your new expectations and standards? With your relationship, work, body, health, money, and contentment? What are you intentionally committing to right now?

Start being honest with yourself about what your old standards were and what new standards you are choosing now.

In every single moment of every single day, we are creating the future.

So it starts today.

What is the life you actually want to start living now?

Or, if you want to ask yourself another question, try this – 'If I was guaranteed that it would work out, what would I change or ask for?'

I also want you to reflect on this – are you still remembering to play in your life, work and business?

Has life just somehow become about functioning and growth, and are you noticing it all feels so serious?

The key thing here is that the magic of life comes when you are finding the joy in the NOW.

When you have a deep and true connection with who you truly are.

When you are playful, open, and curious.

When you approach challenges as the Universe helping to guide you on your highest path.

When you stop making it all about getting somewhere and instead make it about the life you are living.

This means starting to prioritise what brings you alive.

How do you actually want to do life, business, and work right now?

Not because it gets you somewhere but because it feels good right now.

We often wait until the promise of the next level of success to get our dream day in place, spend more time in nature, be more present, and access more joy.

Then the goal posts get moved again.

But success is experiencing those things, right now.

How might things change if that became your focus?

EXERCISE FOR MOMENTUM

Write down the answer to these things:

1. What are five things that would be really nice to have in your life right now? Things that seem a little bit of a stretch but are possible.

2. What are five things that would be incredible to have in your life now? Things that would be magical and you can't comprehend how they would happen.

3. Write down five things that are the BIGGEST things you could ever think to ask for. Things that would just be totally magical and impossible to comprehend if they came into your life. Basically, how big can you ask here?

I then want you to take these 15 things and ask yourself this: 'If I was to make a tiny move towards each one of these things, where would I start?' Then go do it NOW.

If I was guaranteed
that it would work out,
what would I change
or ask for?

ACTUALLY
I CAN

SECTION 2:

Actually, I Can

In order to move forwards, we need to be disciplined in changing the voice from 'What if I can't do this?' to 'Actually, I can'.

These three words have transformed how I see myself, the world, and everything in it.

Like so many, I used to be a serial offender when it came to getting in my own way. My inner critic would create roadblocks, often beginning with the words, 'Oh, but I can't because …'

While the excuses sometimes changed – 'I'm not that person / I don't have any other options / Where would the money come from?' – the negative mindset rarely did. Wherever there was an opportunity, I often buried it with doubts. I knew that I wanted to set up my own business but had ruled it out by convincing myself that it was too big of a risk. That is the thing with inactivity – it's often rooted in a fear of failure. The fear becomes self-fulfilling; we fail because we never start.

I was caught up in a vicious cycle of knowing that I wasn't that happy and yet also telling myself that there wasn't anything I could do about it. I see so many people telling themselves these critical stories, and then I see the magic when clients challenge these stories and believe in themselves.

This is the power of this work, of these three magical words.

Actually, I can.

When you give yourself permission to go for it, you begin to dwell on what you can do – and what you want to do – and not the other way round. What you focus on really does grow.

I've seen it with countless clients …

From a marketing consultant who finally started her dream of becoming a photographer and now photographs the most incredible brands, runs workshops and programs on visibility and who even has a thriving photo club.

From a business development director who left her high-flying job to start illustrating and now has a successful business generating five-figure months and who gets to have flexibility and time with her three children.

From a sports professional who thought his career was over once he finished playing professionally and who has gone to create a successful brand that helps others fulfil their potential.

Whatever it is you want to change about your life, a simple way to start is to introduce these three words into your life: Actually, I can.

Say them, write them, repeat them, and welcome them.

Then sit back and watch as they work their magic.

EXERCISE FOR MOMENTUM

Write down the five things you most desire to change or claim and then write down 'Actually, I can' in front of them.

For example:

Actually, I can be in the best shape of my life.

Actually, I can create an incredible business.

Actually, I can make more money than I ever dreamed was possible.

Actually, I can have an amazing relationship.

Actually, I can become a best-selling author.

Then ask yourself, What are two practical things I could do now to show I believe in these statements?

Whatever it is you
want to change about
your life, a simple way
to start is to introduce
these three words into
your life:
Actually, I can.

LISTEN TO THE FLUTTERINGS OF YOUR HEART

SECTION 3:

Coming into the Heart Over Head

There is immense wisdom in the heart.

We so often disregard matters of the heart because it is all about the feeling.

It is time for you to honour the wisdom of your heart.

What does your heart want to say to you?

What does it need?

What does it yearn for?

Where has your head not allowed your heart to truly express itself?

If you stopped being afraid of listening to it, what does it actually want to say?

Your heart chakra is an incredible portal for receiving guidance, connecting to something greater than you, and allowing love to permeate through all the decisions you make.

Now is the time to re-establish this incredible connection with your heart.

To allow it to speak its truth.

When I was feeling stuck in my corporate job, I knew that my heart was trying to tug at me.

And I ignored it.

The thing is, the heart should get a say too.

It's immensely wise, loving, and powerful.

When you are coming home to you, it is essential you re-establish a connection with your heart and the messages it wants to bring you.

There is so much wisdom in these messages.

A powerful practice that I continually use is to spend a few minutes dropping into my heart and asking her to guide me on where to go next.

From there, I ask myself what action can I take today from the place my heart is guiding me to.

EXERCISE FOR MOMENTUM

Notice how you are identifying with your mind, then take a moment to use your breath to drop into your heart space and feel him/her beneath your hands. Breathe deeper into your heart space.

Take a moment to apologise for not listening to that part of you.

Explain how you want to become close again.

Then, ask the heart to speak with you.

What does he/she want and desire?

Listen and trust.

You may get a word, a feeling, or a pull.

Trust this.

If you feel blocked, simply say out loud or in your head, 'I can, and I am.'

The more you practice this, the more connected you will become.

And as you move forwards, you can ask yourself:

Am I stuck in my head here?

Can I drop into my heart and listen to the whispers instead?

Then what can I actually do practically to create momentum now I've heard this guidance?

LOVE
FEAR
LET LOVE BE YOUR GUIDE

SECTION 4: What Would You Do if You Couldn't Fail?

What would you do if you knew you couldn't fail?

It's an interesting question when we think about it.

Often, fear of failure completely stalls any momentum.

I often see my clients caught up in procrastination, inactivity, or perfectionism – each of these a defence mechanism around fear of failure.

If we don't get going properly, then we believe that we protect ourselves from failure.

The thing is, clarity frequently comes from action.

As we move and do, we often work things out.

When we stop seeing failure as something to be feared but instead see it as something where we learn and grow, then we can stop fearing it so much.

Failure can become one of our greatest teachers rather than something to be avoided at all costs.

EXERCISE FOR MOMENTUM

List out five things that you are putting off doing in case you fail. Then ask yourself what might happen if you do them.

The next thing is to write on a post-it note - do something scary today.

This scary thing should be in the direction of the dream life you want to create - maybe you give up sugar or alcohol, start going to the gym, buy a web domain, reach out to a magazine for some PR, speak to your boss about a pay rise, hire a team member, leave a relationship that doesn't serve you, or travel around the world.

In this moment, consider what could happen if you do something scary but expansive each day for a year - that is 365 big moves in a year.

Imagine where that could take you.

GROWTH IS NOT LINEAR

SECTION 5:

Working With Obstacles

When things feel like they are going wrong, I now view things differently.

Over time, I have coded the belief that everything is conspiring in my favour so that things can work out even more magically than I ever dreamed was possible.

So now when things look like they are going wrong, I see this as the Universe doing me a favour and taking me in a new and even more magical direction.

I also see obstacles as an opportunity to learn.

I ask what this obstacle is trying to:

show me

teach me

guide me

open up for me.

Obstacles are often opportunities in disguise.

They are teachers.

But we so often just see them as blocks.

If you are experiencing a block at the moment – ask yourself this:

Where could I see this as an opportunity instead?

If I had the deep-seated belief this was happening to support me and guide me to my next step – where do I feel I am being called to act?

Is there another door opening here that I am being guided towards?

EXERCISE FOR MOMENTUM

Think of what obstacles you are coming up against now and ask yourself:

How could I view these things differently?

What is it trying to show or teach me?

How could I change my perspective here and see this as an opportunity to shift and grow?

SECTION 6:

Following Your Gut

We have been conditioned away from the belief that we can trust ourselves and our natural instinct to know when we are being guided towards something.

Perhaps you are someone who finds that when you need to make a decision, you ask everyone else for their opinion.

Or you get on social media and look for inspiring quotes or advice from others.

Perhaps you go into your head and look at the facts now.

Taking the time to digest things cerebrally is important. We have a wonderful ability to employ the mind to help us navigate the risks and opportunities in a situation.

But the mind is limited.

Enter in our gut instinct.

With your gut, you have a brilliant ability to go beyond the facts and to start connecting to your inner knowing.

So, when you are honest with yourself, what is your gut telling you?

Where you are you guided?

Let your gut tell you what it wants.

Humour the fact it feels totally 'nuts' and say, 'If I was to act purely on feeling, where am I being guided to go?'

'What am I being guided to see?'

Then ask yourself if you are brave enough to choose from this place.

This section is a call to action.

Please know that …

You never feel ready.

You never know the how.

You never feel enough.

But when we trust ourselves and our internal guidance to know what is right for us, big things can happen.

Your gut feeling on things, people, and situations is incredibly powerful, and if you needed one, this is your permission slip to use it.

EXERCISE FOR MOMENTUM

What is your gut asking you to do that feels loud and clear? Yes, even if it feel scary and irrational.

If you are struggling to connect in, try this exercise:

Ask a question about a decision you need to make and allow your stomach to answer. Go with the immediate answer you are given.

Ask your stomach whether the answer is:

- green (go for it)
- amber (hold off on this for now)
- red (don't do it).

This can be used for big and small decisions – it's a very powerful tool.

BALANCE

SECTION 7:

Having More Balance in Your Life

When we want to create momentum in our lives, it is important to use a combination of both the masculine and feminine energies available to us, rather than a reliance on one over the other.

We are looking for the union of both energies to move us forwards.

The masculine and feminine energies are not about us being male or female; this is about us accessing the different tools that those sets of energies give us.

Both are incredibly important and powerful for finding balance, joy, and contentment and also for creating momentum.

For me, first comes the feminine. The part of me that is connected to my intuition, my creativity, my ability to be with the guidance coming through. Every morning I tune into this energy so I can have her guidance as my compass. Next come the masculine energies, where it is about taking these ideas and desires and moving them forwards – I use my ability to build and strategise and to pull on resiliency and determination here.

As an idea, some of the feminine energies that are available to you are reflection, creativity, emotional guidance, being, heart connection, compassion, sensuality, acceptance. Some of the masculine energies are action-taking, logic, boundaries, objectivity, risk-taking, assertiveness, analysis and discipline.

The thing is, a lot of us rely on the masculine energies, which means we get into a continual state of pushing, striving, fixating on achievement and moving forwards at all costs. On the flip side, we can get stuck in the feminine where we never move forwards, we become passive and stagnant, and are stuck in indecisiveness.

As you are reading this, what is coming up for you in terms of areas where you feel you might be out of balance?

EXERCISE FOR MOMENTUM

Look at where you feel you might be out of balance and see if you can think of something practically that you can do to swap the masculine energy for the feminine or vice versa.

For example:

If you are always on the go, take 10 minutes each day to train yourself to simply be. Set a timer on your phone and practice sitting quietly, looking out the window, or being in nature.

If you are someone who is indecisive and struggles to move forwards, ask yourself where you could take some forward action. Practice disciplining yourself into doing something small each day to move things forward. Again, I would recommend setting up a reminder on your phone to make sure you actually do this.

SECTION 8:
Connecting to Something Greater Than You

There is something greater than you at play.

There is a Universal intelligence that governs everything.

You have access to it, you are part of it, you are made up of it.

When you commit to co-creating with it, seriously magical things happen.

Connecting to the Universe means operating with an energy that is outside of your thoughts, your conditioning, and what seemingly feels possible.

You can't necessarily see it, but that does not make it not real.

By connecting with something greater than you, the Universe is going to ask you to transcend the limits of your ego and to operate from a place of deep trust and connection.

I like to look at the Universe as a great friend that is constantly championing me.

It wants me to have everything I desire and more; it knows my greatness and it knows that my every wish is its command.

The thing is, the Universe needs me to do my thing.

It needs me to:

- ask for what I actually want rather than what I don't want
- do any inner work that is blocking me from believing it is possible
- be open to receiving the guidance that can fulfil this wish and then being open to taking any action that may be needed
- receive, with arms open wide, everything that I have asked for whenever that decides to come

However, we forget these fundamental Universal laws work if we trust they do.

Instead, we default to making it happen ourselves, pushing, watching the clock for when it might arrive and then obsessing over the 'how'.

The Universe is quite clear – the 'how' is not our business.

If you want to start calling in your dream life, start focusing less on how it comes together and instead focus on becoming clear about what it is you are asking for, trusting any guidance that comes through, and relinquishing the need to control.

It's then that your trusted mate, the Universe, can blow your socks off by doing its thing.

Since I started out on this journey, it's had to come down to an unshakeable faith that it will work out.

That I am guided, that it is going to be okay.

All those times, I have followed a hunch that has led me to where I am now despite having no proof.

I now realise it has brought me exactly the right people, circumstances and events.

Ultimately, I do trust, with all my being, that I am hugely supported. That I can completely trust myself and where I am guided. That I can trust that everything is ultimately going to work out. That everything is conspiring in my favour.

I know with certainty that when I choose and act and make my moves from my soul, then a series of extraordinary events occur to get me to the position I find myself in now.

And the thing is, this business was never a given.

But somehow, deep inside, I believed it was.

And I trusted that feeling with all my being.

EXERCISE FOR MOMENTUM

In order to start building trust, we need to practice it.

So this is where I want you to start asking for guidance from the Universe.

I want you to start trusting that there is a power greater than you guiding you.

Here are some things that can help:

- Ask the Universe to bring you clarity, to guide you, to help you with anything that you struggling with as you go to sleep at night. Set the expectation that you wake with a new sense of perspective

- Continually ask the Universe to guide you if anything needs to be done, and when you get the nudge (as weird and unrelated as it seems), honour it

- Write a Universal to-do list – yes, give the Universe a set of 'jobs' and trust it will deliver. Avoid the need to check – you have been heard

- Take a moment each day to close your eyes and ask for what you want; visualise having it already and feel the feelings of gratitude right now for it being done. Imagine sending this vision and request to the Universe in a pink bubble that floats off into space and is heard. Then forget about it, trust it is on its way, and do anything that you are given the nudge to do in the meantime

SECTION 9:

Your Higher Self

Every one of us has access to a higher-self version of us.

Think of it like an incredible, badass, alter ego.

They are formidable. A force. Wise. Loving. Knowing.

All the good things.

This higher self is a part of you that somehow has it all together, and guess what – they are here on standby to help whenever you need them to guide you.

They see beyond the freak-out, the dramas, the not enough-ness, the limitations, and they are a very powerful guide for you. So how do we access this part of us and bring all this incredible guidance through?

For me, I ask myself what the person who is living her dream life and running her dream business looks, feels, and sounds like.

I ask myself what are her beliefs, her stories, her habits, and her way of operating her day.

I then get really clear on what that would look like, and I tune into the energy of her and ask what decisions she would make in this moment, how she would view this block, how she would address a certain situation.

I ask her to make decisions for me.

Think of it like this: say you see the future-you as this incredible thought-leader and speaker who is having a global impact. When you connect to their energy, you start to show up like that right now. You start speaking and leading with more power, impact, and radiance. Then all of a sudden more people listen, and your audience grows. People are responding to the new energy you are holding, and before you know it, you have created the reality that was once a vision.

EXERCISE FOR MOMENTUM

Get clear on what your future self is like. Use all of the criteria I have listed above. Then ask how you can start bringing that person into your life now.

Can they show up for you now?

Make decisions for you now?

What does your higher self want you to start owning, claiming and deciding now?

SECTION 10:

Showing Up for Yourself

As we come to the end of this book, I want you to know that you and you alone get to decide that you are showing up for yourself.

You have a choice when you put this book down to go back to the previous way of doing and being or to make a decision to take total accountability and responsibility for the life you are creating.

It is today that you get to stop asking for permission to create your dream life and instead step up as the incredible magician you are and take complete responsibility for being the powerful creator of your reality.

This takes guts to do.

It takes guts to trust a feeling over logic.

It takes guts to listen to your intuition and take action from there.

It takes guts to believe in an energy and connection that you can't physically see.

It takes guts to create the space to let the magic in.

But when you do so, everything can change for you.

I mean, seriously, what are we all doing?

The negotiating, the bargaining, the scarcity.

The belief we are too greedy, we are not worthy, it's too much.

Not wanting to be too much, ask for too much, desire too much, receive too much.

This has to stop.

We are supposed to expand. We are supposed to shine brightly. We are supposed to focus on the truth of all that we are and all that we came here to do.

We are supposed to tap into our desires and dreams, and then leap so fully into the belief that we can have them that we become unstoppable.

Please know: that greatness you feel and see inside of you ... that is your TRUTH.

Welcome back home to you.

Inspirational Stories From My Clients

I have been in Caroline's world since November 2020. Actually, her name came to me via a mutual friend in the summer of 2019, but as the Universe would have it, we weren't meant to meet until some time later! Back to November 2020 … I had just been signed off work sick for a month with anxiety and exhaustion. I'd love to say this was the first time, but unfortunately, it was not an unfamiliar situation to me. I had experienced 'burnout' several times over the years in my leadership and executive roles both in the UK and in the UAE, yet this time something was distinctly different. I had been on a path of spiritual awakening for the two years prior, from devouring every self-help book I could get my hands on to daily meditation, energy clearing and psychic readings. So, when this big crash came in November 2020, I knew in my heart it was a big red

STOP sign from the Universe. My soul wanted me to listen. It was time.

I had lost myself in the world of 'shoulds', 'must dos', and 'have tos' (so easily done for so many of us). I had lost who I was and I had most definitely lost my way to what really made me happy, feel deeply fulfilled and abundant in all areas of my life. It was in this moment on the sofa, sleeping my way to recovery, that Caroline's name dropped in again. I checked out her website, sent her a voice note, and that was that! I joined a programme she was running called Mastery of Manifestation which opened my eyes to the reality of co-creating my desires with the Universe. Miracles started to happen, including manifesting our dream house! With Caroline's help, I dedicated myself to tapping into my inner calling and purpose as a Soul-Led Leadership Coach, helping others to listen to their soul and create a career and life in which they thrive and grow. I learnt about the power of working with the quantum, and I added to my traditional coaching qualification by certifying within her coaching academy as an Intuitive Coach, truly embracing my own gifts. In June 2021, I took the biggest leap of my life, followed Soul and left my 20+ year corporate career to be an entrepreneur. This was not a small decision; at the time, I was the main income earner in our family, but it was the RIGHT decision, and with Caroline's help as a private client of hers by that point, I locked that belief in, made the step and haven't looked back since.

Knowing who I am, who I came here to be, and choosing that I do get to have the life I desire, that I get to serve soul-aligned clients in a business that lights me up and that I get to do my part in changing the world for the better is a gift and a path that I couldn't have imagined that I would get to walk. Yet here I am! And if I can do it, anyone can! I'm not going to pretend it's easy, the fears and worries and need to take care of myself continue to come, but I know I can hold that, and I have seen and continue to see the magic on the other side of working through any obstacles. Transformation happens on the other side of challenges when we believe in who we are and why we are here. Every time! Working with Caroline has changed my life. She helps to make the miraculous happen, and I will be forever grateful!

Stacy Holland, Stacy Holland Coaching

In November 2019, life was pretty great. A happy home, three amazing children and a beautiful business ... but something was deeply out of kilter. I was running a business in the body of a workaholic.

Tired, annoyed, and in a hamster wheel of feeling that no matter how hard I worked, nothing would move forward … stuck in a perpetual pattern of undercharging and overworking (sound familiar?).

On a hunch and a nudge from a friend, I booked a meeting with Caroline. 'One sesh should "fix me",' I thought to myself, and besides, what sort of person invests in themselves like this … wasn't it all just a bit self-indulgent?

Walking into that little cafe in North London, this petite, big-eyed young woman greeted me with a hug and so much warmth. *Does she know me already?* I wondered.

We didn't speak about work. I quickly understood that this was going to be about my 'energy', the stories I held around money, the beliefs about myself, and in turn, every area of my life. She shone this bright, compassionate and magical torch into the darkest recesses of my spirit. An hour after our session, I received a call from a new client … this was going to be a completely different project for the business, and it didn't take a second for me to connect the dots. A few weeks later, another opportunity showed up. What. Was. Happening?

That single session has transformed into three years of journeying into joy. Caroline, in all her beauty, has cheered me on and challenged me using her special mix of kindness, magic and straight-talking. I've cried (quite a bit), been really brave, rewired my habits of exhaustion to make way for fun, rest, laughter and, yes, the business is also unrecognisable.

How good can it get? is my revised life mantra. In truth, I've only just started, but so has Caroline …

Angela Simpson, Simpson and Voyle

What is next

If you desire to take this work deeper, I recommend looking at my variety of online and live programs listed at www.caroline-britton.com

You can also find a selection of free programs and teachings under www.caroline-britton.com / free-resources-1

To follow me on Instagram, head to @carolinebrittoncoaching

To join my Private Facebook Group, head to www.facebook.com / groups / carolinebritton

Acknowledgments

I want to take a moment to thank everyone who has been involved in bringing this book to life.

To Matt, Mum and Dad for your unwavering support, love and belief in me. My rocks.

To Brother Ian, thanks for keeping me grounded and having my back. True words.

To Claudia and Harry, you are beyond magical. The gift that keeps giving. Thank you for being you.

To my family, thank you for your unconditional love and laughter.

To Tsunako - thank you for everything and for being so truly excellent at what you do. I love being on this adventure with you.

To my incredible group of friends for the play, the cheerleading and being the powerhouses you are.

To Nicola and the team at Unbound Press who made the journey of writing my first book an experience full of joy and support.

To my support team of coaches, mentors, healers and guides - thank you for appearing at the perfect time and for guiding me to my highest self each time.

To my clients for believing I was the woman to walk with you and for showing me what is possible when you come home to you.

And finally to my spirit squad - I couldn't do this without you. Thank you for everything.

About Caroline Britton

Caroline Britton is a global speaker, teacher, coach, mentor, healer, and intuitive guide, and an expert in helping people connect back to their soul.

Alongside a background of 14 years in a global consultancy, Caroline is a Mum of two and described as a 'magic-maker' by those who work with her.

Caroline delivers her powerful teachings through a combination of online courses, private coaching and speaking events and works with a variety of clients from sports professionals, CEOs, entrepreneurs, healers, working professionals, and those in the public eye.

Caroline has been featured in Forbes, The Telegraph, GQ, Red Magazine and numerous other publications.

For more information on Caroline, head to www.caroline-britton.com

Printed in Great Britain
by Amazon

81804354R00142